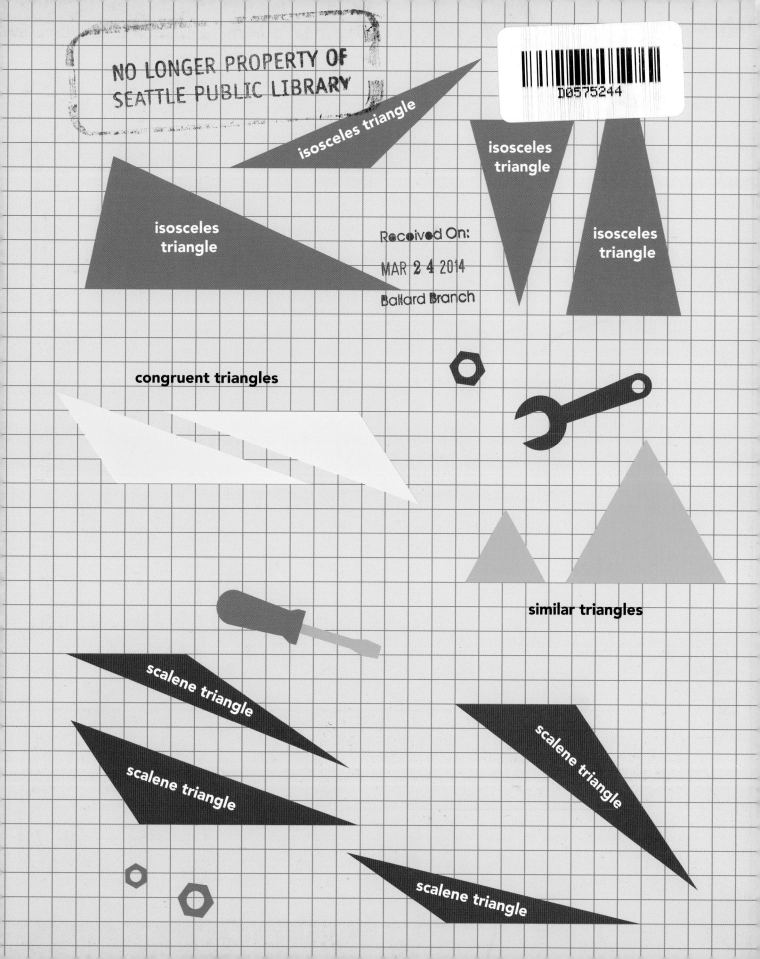

isosceles triangle

isosceles triangle

isosceles triangle

isosceles triangle

congruent triangles

similar triangles

scalene triangle

scalene triangle

scalene triangle

scalene triangle

TRIANGLES

by **David A. Adler** · illustrated by **Edward Miller**

Holiday House / New York

Make three dots on a sheet of paper. The dots should not be in a straight line. Use a ruler as a guide and connect the dots.

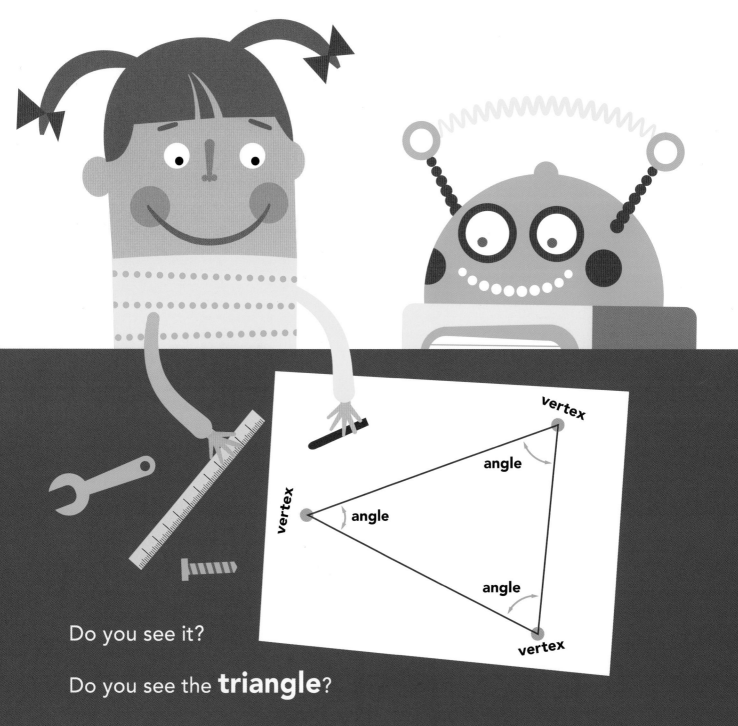

vertex

angle

vertex

angle

angle

vertex

Do you see it?

Do you see the **triangle**?

A triangle is a flat, closed figure with just three sides.

Draw lots of dots, lots of lines, and lots of triangles.

Each triangle has three sides. Each triangle also has three **angles**. An angle is what's made when two straight lines meet. The two lines are the sides of the angle.

The point where they meet is called the **vertex**.

Look around this room.
There are lots of lines.
Do you see lots of angles?
Do you see lots of triangles?
Angles and triangles are everywhere.

Angles have names.

The name of this angle is ABC.

The name of this angle is LMN.

Three letters are used to name an angle. The center letter is always the vertex.

Here's an analog clock with two hands, an hour hand, and a minute hand. At noon both hands point to 12.

As the time passes, the minute hand moves quickly around the dial. The hour hand moves more slowly. The two hands form an angle.

Do you see it?

Do you see the angle made by the clock's two hands?

As the hands move, the angle changes.

As the minutes pass, the distance between the two hands of the clock gets greater. The greater the distance between the two hands, the larger the angle.

The size of an angle is measured in degrees.

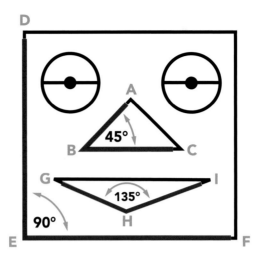

<ABC (angle ABC) is 45° (45 degrees).

<DEF is 90°.

<GHI is 135°.

This tool is called a protractor. It is used to measure angles.

The < means "angle."
The ° means "degrees."

Angles go from 0° to 360°. Every circle has 360°.

An angle that is less than 90° is called an **acute angle**.

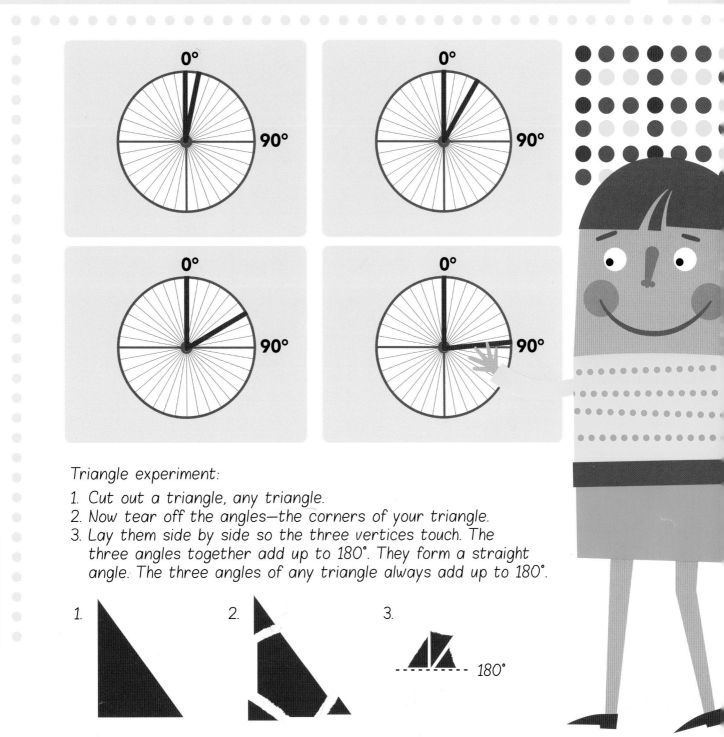

Triangle experiment:

1. Cut out a triangle, any triangle.
2. Now tear off the angles—the corners of your triangle.
3. Lay them side by side so the three vertices touch. The three angles together add up to 180°. They form a straight angle. The three angles of any triangle always add up to 180°.

An angle that is exactly 90° is called a **right angle**.
You see right angles at the corners of every square and rectangle.

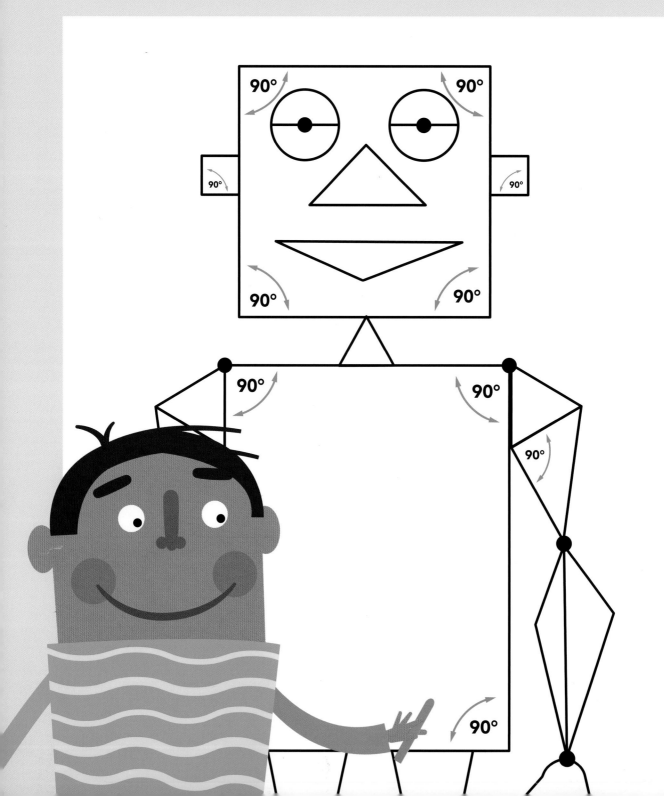

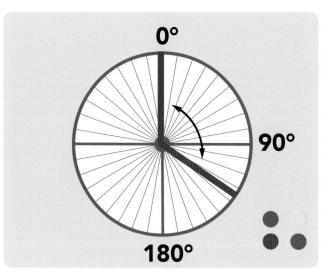

An angle from 90° to 180° is called an **obtuse angle**.

An angle that is exactly 180° is called a **straight angle**.

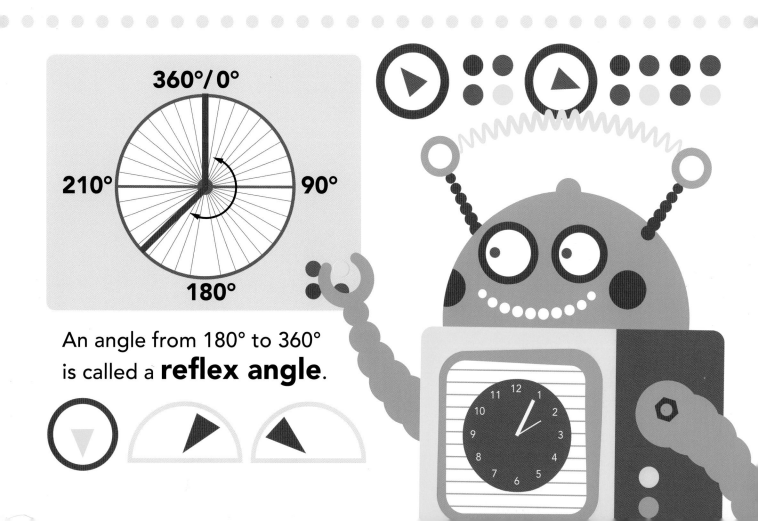

An angle from 180° to 360° is called a **reflex angle**.

Triangles also have names.

Triangles are named according to the sizes of their angles.

Here are lots of triangles.

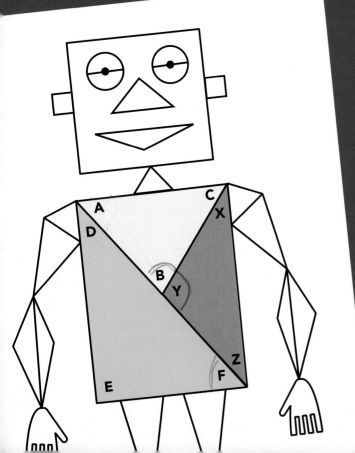

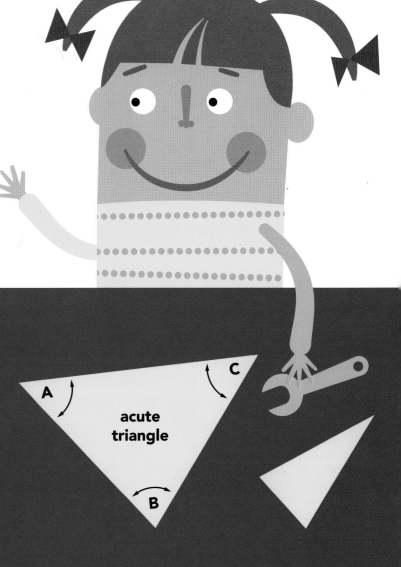

acute
triangle

All three angles in △ABC (triangle ABC) are acute angles. △ABC is an **acute triangle**.

One angle in ΔDEF (triangle DEF) is a right angle.
ΔDEF is a **right triangle**.

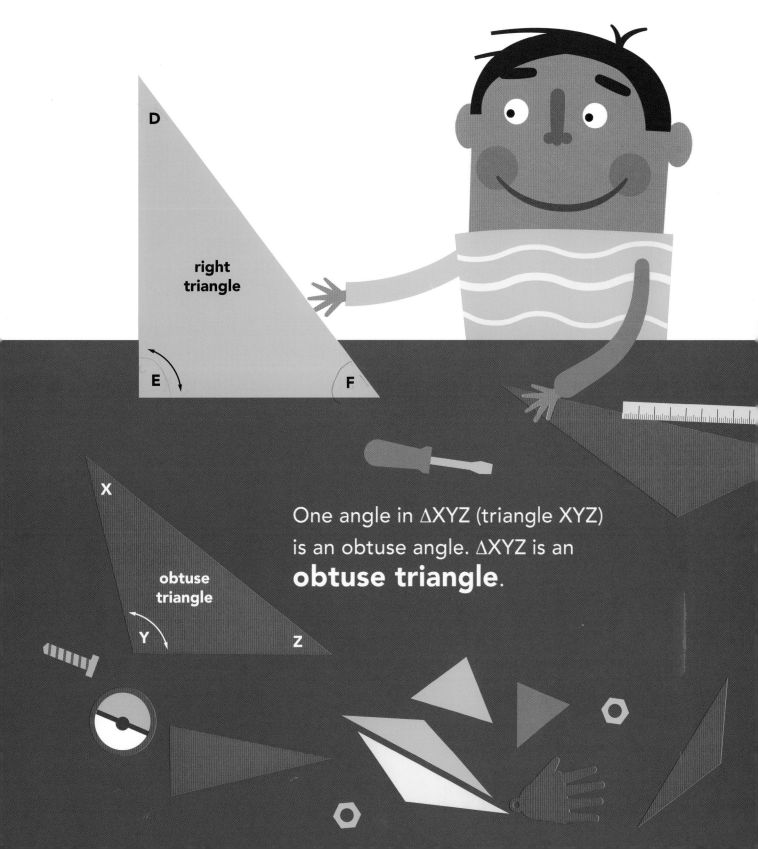

right
triangle

One angle in ΔXYZ (triangle XYZ)
is an obtuse angle. ΔXYZ is an
obtuse triangle.

obtuse
triangle

Triangles are also named according to the relative length of their sides.

Here are lots of triangles.

Do you see a triangle in which all three sides are the exact same length? That's an **equilateral triangle**.

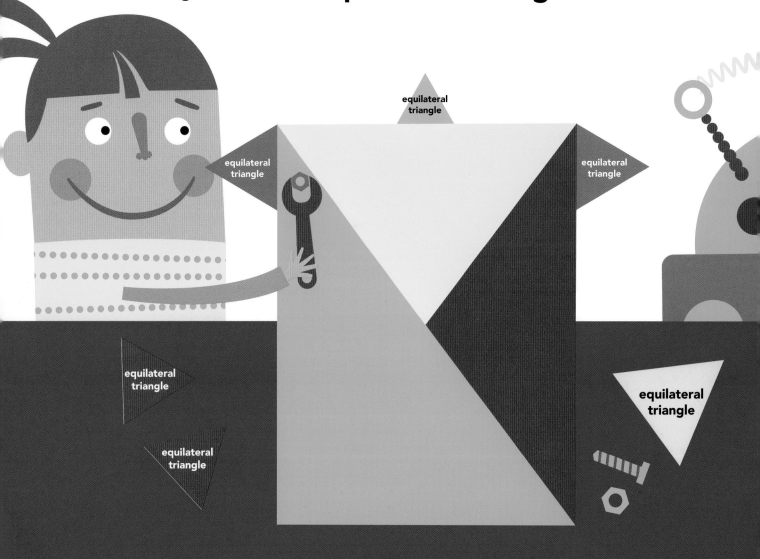

equilateral triangle

equilateral triangle

equilateral triangle

equilateral triangle

equilateral triangle

equilateral triangle

Look at the angles of the equilateral triangle. If all the sides are the same length, all the angles are the same size.

Do you see a triangle in which two sides are the exact same length? That's an **isosceles triangle**.

In an isosceles triangle the angles opposite the two equal sides are also equal.

Do you see a triangle in which all three sides are different lengths? That's a **scalene triangle**.

Look at the scalene triangle.

The smallest side is opposite the smallest angle of the triangle.

The largest side is opposite the largest angle. All three sides of a scalene triangle are different. All three angles are also different.

smallest side

scalene triangle

smallest angle

smallest side

scalene triangle

largest side

scalene triangle

largest angle

smallest side

scalene triangle

largest side

scalene triangle

largest angle

Are you a good triangle detective?

Look at these triangles. Do you see any two that are the same shape? If they're the same shape, the measure of their three angles is the same. Triangles with the same shape—the same sized angles—are said to be **similar**.

Look at these triangles again. Do you see any two that are exactly the same? Triangles with angles and sides that are the same sizes are said to be **congruent**.

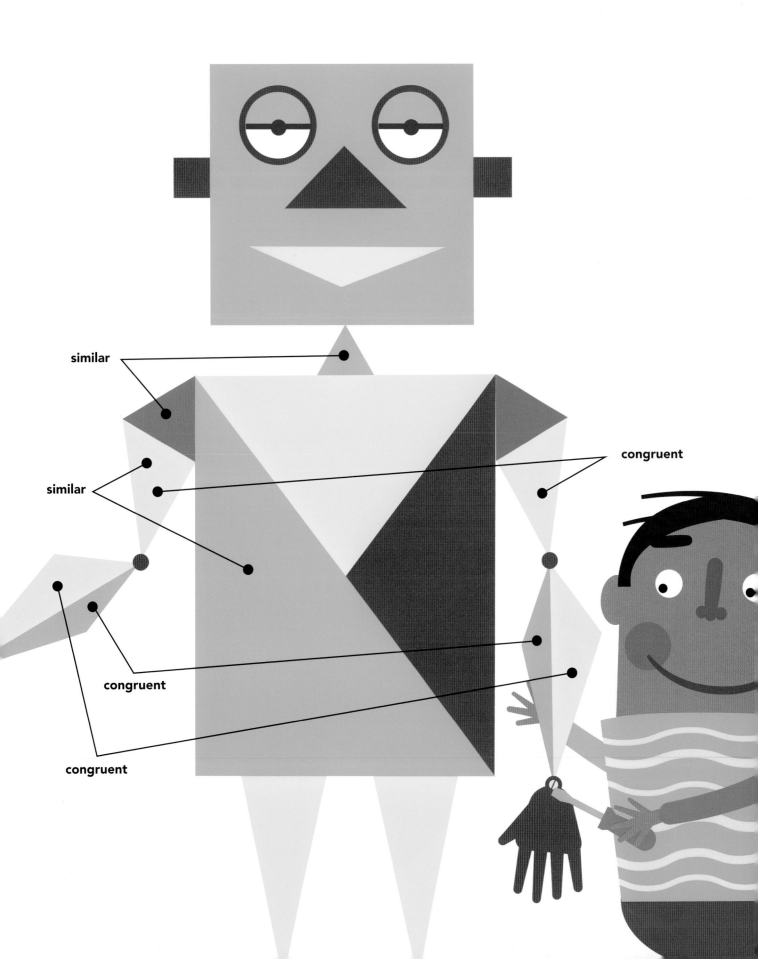

similar

similar

congruent

congruent

congruent

congruent

Bend your arm.

Do you see an angle?

Hold up your hand.

Spread your fingers apart.

Do you see any angles?

Your lower arm and upper arm form an angle. Your elbow is the vertex of the angle.

Can you find any acute angles?

Can you find any right angles?

Can you find any obtuse angles?

Be on the lookout for angles and triangles everywhere you go.

(Turn the page for the answers.)

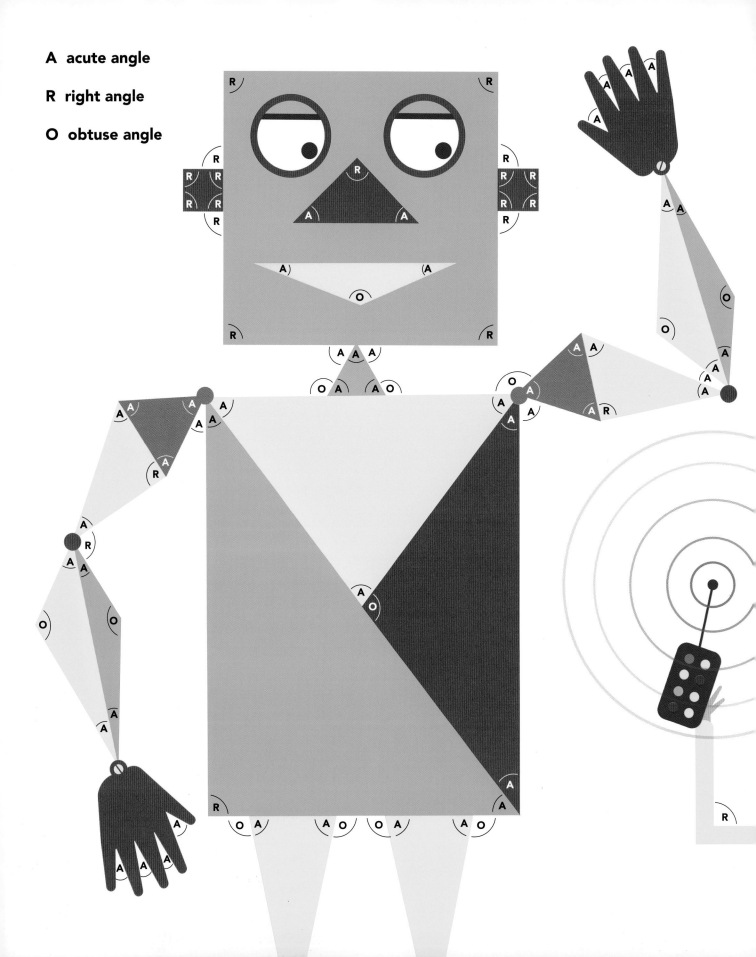

A acute angle

R right angle

O obtuse angle

For Michael and Deborah—D. A. A.

In memory of my art teacher Florence M. McCarthy—E. M.

Text copyright © 2014 by David A. Adler
Illustrations copyright © 2014 by Edward Miller III
All Rights Reserved
HOLIDAY HOUSE is registered in the U.S. Patent and Trademark Office.
Printed and Bound in November 2013 at Toppan Leefung, DongGuan City, China.
www.holidayhouse.com
First Edition
1 3 5 7 9 10 8 6 4 2

Library of Congress Cataloging-in-Publication Data

Adler, David A.
Triangles / by David A. Adler ; illustrated by Edward Miller. — First edition.
pages cm
Audience: Age 4-8.
Audience: Grade K to grade 3.
ISBN 978-0-8234-2378-1 (hardcover)
1. Triangle—Juvenile literature. I. Miller, Edward, 1964- illustrator. II. Title.
QA482.A35 2014   516'.154—dc23   2012037371

Visit www.davidaadler.com for more information on the author, for a list of his books, and to download teacher's guides and educational materials. You can also learn more about the writing process, take fun quizzes, and read select pages from David A. Adler's books.

**This books meets the Common Core Standards for Mathematics for fifth grade: 5.G.3 & 4:
Classify two-dimensional figures into categories based on their properties.**

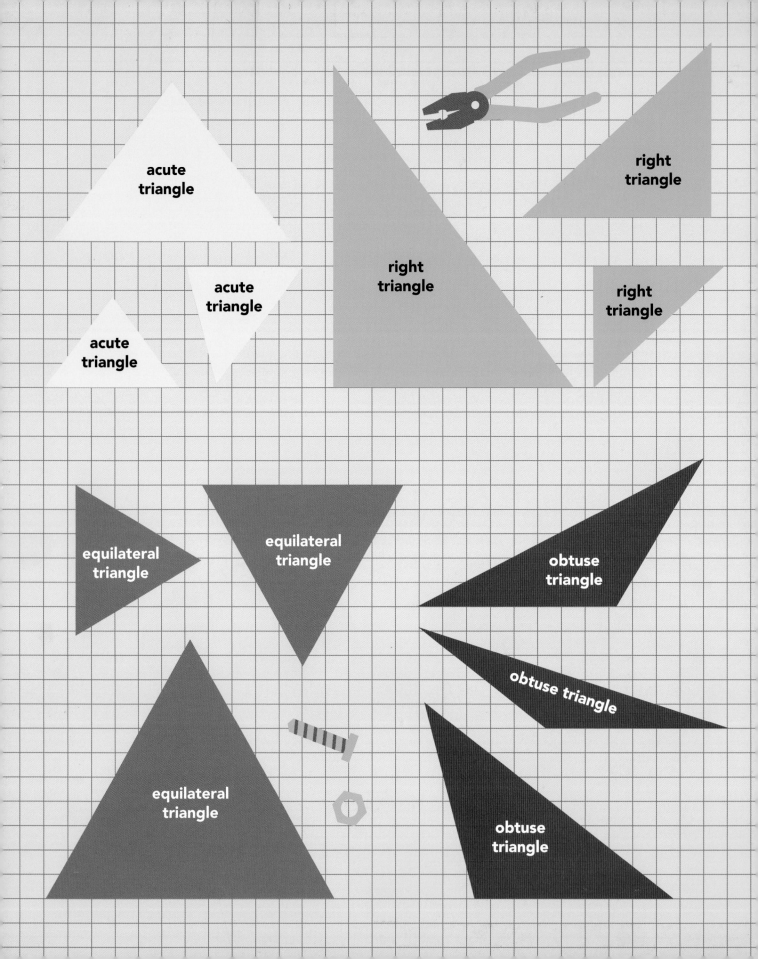